A LAST TEAR EVER CRIED.

JAY SAXENA

POETRY AND MUSIC BEING A SALVATION,
TO STARVING SOUL, FOUND IT; SHALL REST IN PEACE.

RHYTHM AND WORDS
A PLATFORM FOR POETRY AND MUSIC,
COMMEMORATING GOOD MEMORIES OF A HEARTBREAK

TO INKED SOUL; A STAGE TO SPEAK

Contents

Contents

A Last Tear Ever Cried.
Jay Saxena.

Preface

"A Last Tear Ever Cried." To describe the book in shades of lilacs, transition to a gravely grey, an August to un-write and a memory to swirl in parch'd August dry. Poems about an intersection where They chose "...Till death and beyond" And bisexuality to run away and fall in the crevices made by patriarchy. Infidelity a goodbye to the gay of poet, and happiness to destiny destined to be.

Phases of poet, where he chooses to love, to hate, gets anxious, gets insecure about the relationship. An anxious feeling ignites through, and infidelity runs parallel to the monogamy.

Acknowledgements

To be acknowledged, are no one; but those who heard me muffled in those pillows; late at night, heard me for the vulnerability that were been carried by me in the voices, through the day, the night-fall and all those sickening anxiety spirals of loosing someone.

Even the acknowledged here are those, who have far gone; and have no relatibility to the life of me, to the senses I breathe in world apart from poetry.

Prologue

"*Nowhere now my heart goes,*
Everyone else's eyes judge me,
Everything I do, Elevates from it's meaning,
Levitates from it's life, always left demeaned,
Powerful pen, my poetries are poison,
All of em' disagree, but;
Wrapped safe, round in your arms,
Axis and allies means nothing when;
Revival and my restoration happens in your arms."

is a soliloquy spoken, to myself in the midnights of monday nights, in covid; where all would hast been a nightmare to say the least but the spoken words were a fragment of each and all from anger to the lust and a mourn of loosing love, in the spirals of anxiety.

I

Seventh Of March.

Steps, thereof, I shall never forget,

Carnations and lilies, burning,

Darkness un-prevailed,

Quarrel of lights, naked, embroidered in scars,

Thereof, a crown, I shan't let it fall,

Rains in March, oddly, a guilt satisfaction, to us,

Steps, thereof, I shall never forget,

Stars drawn, round my, knit imagination,

Decor that corridor of light,

Soul of this body left, you were so right,

Carnations and lilies burning,

Desires, of disruption, in kingdom my lord,

Satire, by scars of emotions too scarce,

By the bodies, therefore, walked, afar,

Darkness un-prevailed,

Us two, on that bed, starting a story,

Vengeance of unpronounced darkness, of my body,

Aboarded in sail, to your royal kingdom, brain,

Quarrel of lights, naked, embroidered in scars,

Modern love story, would let, leave bodies in dark,

Seventh of March, shall, never taste bitter,

Until what goes by, comes as sweet, my lord,

Thereof, a crown, I shan't let it fall,

Relation of perfection with misogyny,

Let burns, thereby all,

I will hold on till I die, I won't forget us at all.

II

Dark City and The Deserted Road.

I have no one to cling upon,

When I walk back to my house,

I have no one to see in the eyes and smile,

When I walk back to my house,

I have an empty bed,

When I walk back to my house,

It's a black city and a deserted road,

Falling blood and a beating heart,

Safe comfy chest and hot breath amidst lips,

That pulls my worries apart,

Moonlight midst the rain,

Perfection stuck with misogyny,

Irony, of someone young failing again and again,

You're the dark city and I'm the deserted road,

Couplets of bass drums,

On the empty roads of the city,

Hands down, entangled,

Enchanted, every little second,

Touch of your learned hand turns, water

In this deserted road,

Finally, I get someone to cling upon,

Look into his eyes and surrender my happiness,

As the treasure of his empire,

I have an empty bed but a content heart,

That's what happens when

Deserted road meets the dark city,

Of heart beats.

And rain puts it's dryness apart.

III

Dark Room Probation.

A sound from my reverberating vocal chords,

Is sigh,

Cry for time that long waited, rather held;

In my clenched fist, beautiful and grace,

Black in landscape thereby,

Definite mortal shall exist,

Midst those being immortal,

Till my scars shine deep deep blue,

I will exist till I lose hope and feelings too,

Far, farther, farthest landscape covered in black,

Feels like a probation,

Supervisor!? Nowhere to be found,

Scars on my body, shall be inspection to revolutionary,

Black in landscape thereby,

Probation it be,

Stood still, there where I saw myself,

Bleeding wounds shall narrate my profound poem,

Describing, honors left crumbled,

Three words, like I just mumbled,

Forsaken, a slave to my heart,

Been carried around,

Being tormented isn't a phase, my lord,

It's a dark room probation,

Black in landscape thereby,

Where mortals be breathing in fear,

Till decades to pass by.

IV

Poet Of Chaos Theory.

Overturn the ashes of the burnt,

Fire shall not harm me more,

Than what I feel, would an adjective, thereby,

Been attributed, would you still stay, awhile!?

Emotions, a blizzard,

Hostage to feelings,

Unsung fears, mares to bow forward on,

Cacophonies, a prominent chaos, making me feel disdain,

Broken mirror pieces,

Gloomed, in exile, of fears,

Delusion, was sanity, of what I called illusion,

Their perception reflected my identity,

Imagery, of a psycho,

Knit in adjectives,

would you still stay, awhile!?

Poet of a chaos theory,

What's left there to accuse me of!?

Even if it is,

would you still stay, awhile!?

V

Suffocation.

I walk by the room,

With irrelevance of my existence in your life,

A closure, holding the fear,

Of the instance I used to fright from,

Post the hallway,

My tears and I submerge into your hall,

Fairy lights, fading you and I,

Dancing to that one slow song,

You, yet be my dear,

But 'Our' hallucinations would be dearest,

To my heart, which you won't be touching,

Can you calm it down, by your existence,

Don't you feel suffocated!?

When my anxious heart is uncontrollable,

Don't you feel it's toxic,

When my insecurities are unbearable,

Don't you feel the suffocation!?

VI

Golden.

Baffled, in stitches of changing,

Twined in August pale,

Sepia of vintage learnt, hard things to unlearn,

Midst of anguish, Messiah of smoke,

Stood long gainst' angst,

Melancholy of cacophony, through my burns red,

Baffled, in stitches of changing,

Round' on toss, tumbled, a wait, so long,

Weigh of their generosity, thrusted my shoulders,

Indebted to given time, remarks even to my ink,

Twined in August pale,

To wish nothing but them, as friends,

And your hand to kiss, a wish, to bail,

Boulevard of tears, and them to heal a pain,

Sepia of vintage learnt, hard things to unlearn,

Wide imagination narrowed to reality,

Burden of untold future, to hold by all,

Vintage of learnt, things now hard to unlearn,

Midst of anguish, Messiah of smoke,

Highness of burning coal you,

I Stood long gainst' angst,

Melancholy of cacophony, through my burns red,

To wish nothing but them, as friends,

And your hand to kiss, a wish, to bail.

VII

So It Goes.

Far away, where life, rattles,

Beneath the august dried leaves,

And god pronounces trust, a defeat,

So here shall I proceed,

So it goes,

In less than a collision of vision,

So it goes,

Hefty debt, shoulders thrusted,

Off here so goes of attributions,

Of someone's dead love, motionless,

Reasons shall leave you awake for an eternity,

So it goes,

An eternity of awaken soul, reason!?

So it goes,

Midnight moon,

Poisonous hostage to one's own feelings,

Sleeping with a dried body,

His lover, sleeping with same,

Freezing December cold,

While just November bought august pain,

Slight you bow to what's dead,

Reasons, shall let you sleep, but as sound as death,

So it goes,

November of pains, dryness of August,

Made me feel disdain,

So it goes,

Bare what's in the way,

Should let you going,

Would let you stuck on the same,

So it goes, a story to my bane,

So it goes.

VIII

The Interlude poem.

Gaining sympathy,

Our stars aren't alike,

Karma be action of nature to you,

Sigh of relief, revenge be to me,

I shall step down to,

Plead, beg and please,

Your glee, to own him, is your win,

A rid, for him, from this disease,

Mirrors thereby sing harmonies,

Hypnotizing melodies,

And there shall be me, inflicted by the rhythm,

Tears, and mosaic vision.

IX

Intersection.

At the end of it all,

They chose "...Till death and beyond"

For perfection once met, fallen for misogyny,

Misogyny had no mind of its own,

Hearts intersected, beyond and farther,

Forever, and beyond, both misogyny and beauty, fell for the one,

Admire the paradise, at intersection,

Sidelining faith, off the feeling, of love,

Of the mainstream stereotypes,

Wonders of love, left like sandcastle, on shore,

What's there about love, with a whore,

I'm stereotyped about, the misogyny, I proclaimed, myself as,

And the beauty, of vows, between man and woman, thereby,

Beauty, a woman, I envy, now on and about,

Intersection, at my man of interest,

Laid me back time, in quicksand, for he had no choice either,

...Till death and beyond,

Yet ties no knot, to just, vowed or un-vowed,

Statement said with feelings matter,

And if I ever felt, I would show up,

At the intersection, paradise of perfection,

Pedestal someone else living upon,

But till there I be alive, I vow, to

A last tear I ever cry,

I'll show up at the imperfections of time,

With my heart and mind.

X

Perfect.

Misery twined uphold, beheld by mistake,

Black underwear, tears, vision a lens flare,

Regret, remorse, alive, breath a threat,

Infatuation serenade skies, off stolen smile,

Gasping, blood clot on my heart,

Grace, weep silences of already quiten night,

Misery twined uphold, beheld by mistake,

Cyclones, whirling, love amidst,

Twined by misery, upheld by mistake,

Weighing deeper, all burrowed are feelings,

Black underwear, tears, vision a lens flare,

Mosaic vision, tears, trapped love hit glass,

Black underwear, camouflage, in dark,

Touch instructs, knuckles and knees bruised,

Regret, remorse, alive, breath a threat,

Reimburse my heart, in feelings,

To remorse, now regret, a life,

Breath a threat,

Infatuation serenade skies, off stolen smile,

He's perfect, may I should be too,

Was I like a wasted dream!?

To kiss, while I blindfolded, and you were naked, with him,

Gasping, blood clot on my heart,

Grace, weeps in silences of already quieten night,

Gasp, while profundity, in dripping blood,

Grace, wept, silences did sing elegies in quite of night.

XI

A Dreadful Repercussion.

For sake of my skin, to not to bleed,

You shall walk away by the window,

Fall into the sky, fly away in the autumn dry,

Be there where thousand leaves await,

You are off, not by a lane, But by the road,

Your soul been distress, round about dancing,

In front of the right audience,

But on the wrong stage,

For sake of my skin, to not to bleed,

Please walk away,

Bind his feelings, to blind his caretakers,

Your intentions has been evil,

To wind I shall curse to bring you here!?

Or to you, who isn't mature enough to leave!?

You are a belonging,

To which love let's itself loose too soon,

Your actions are sins,

To which my love builds too strong,

For sake of my skin, to not to bleed,

Please walk away,

If dreadful repercussions to my mistakes were you,

If would've been aware of,

I would axe my own grave,

Welcome everyone to my funeral,

But still would've pleaded you,

For sake of my skin, to not to bleed,

But to please walk away.

XII

Disturbia.

Twice tears out open eye,

Hurricane hitting shores, lilac,

Sores affirming death, scars august dry,

Reasons thirteenth march a night,

Elsewhere no hands to slide, in eyes,

Mine skies, mine ocean waves, ours love,

August dry scars, death affirming to, reasons,

Thirteenth march a night,

Hurricane hitting shores, lilac,

Disturbia, of many emotions to lilac as sweet sky,

Distant, august to November to lifelong touch,

Hurricane distress of you, in mistress of my master,

He'd had me twice tears out open eye,

To once of his touch, to another to you,

Means of a master of my skin long gone,

To someone he love calls mistress to you,

Elsewhere no hands to slide, in eyes,

Mine skies, mine ocean waves, ours love,

To all gone last August, to all let undone,

To all lost, to all I be best man of honor.

Twice tears out open eye,

Hurricane hitting shores, lilac,

Sores affirming death, scars august dry,

Reasons thirteenth march a night,

Elsewhere no hands to slide, in eyes,

Mine skies, mine ocean waves, ours love,

August dry scars, death affirming to, reasons,

Thirteenth march a night,

Hurricane hitting shores, lilac,

Disturbia, of many emotions to lilac as sweet sky,

Distant, august to November to lifelong touch,

Hurricane distress of you, in mistress of my master,

He'd had me twice tears out open eye,

To once of his touch, to another to you,

Means of a master of my skin long gone,

To someone he love calls mistress to you,

Elsewhere no hands to slide, in eyes,

Mine skies, mine ocean waves, ours love,

To all gone last August, to all let undone,

To all lost, to all I be best man of honor.

XIII

Wine and Lube.

My intoxication,

Was thirst for wine,

Blind black, skin confined,

Red, of last night, maroon the next morning,

Pale blood, on white sheets,

And feelings infinite,

Drill on an undefined road,

But we ran on a highway,

Lights went off,

And that's when the suspense was rising,

His fingers slided, then serpentined,

Fist literally held my heart,

And my body defied my brain,

Heart held that lube, hopes; for a forever game,

Nothing of it all lasted for just fourth five,

Minutes after it all, he kissed me,

What the odds of it all,

Mirror sky, saw us dancing softly,

Tip toeing licking his lips gently,

Smile, indemnified, silence,

Vision of endless ecstasy,

Echoes, in solid blue,

Hands tangled just like we did under,

Thousand glowing moons,

I remember a silhouette, smoking,

Pushing my head between his legs,

Up-thrusting himself in me,

Pure, vulnerable and deep,

You are silence, a dried forest of August,

Would've been before me,

Would've heard him moan,

Now only when he will, he ought to think of me.

XIV

Best Man and The god.

Elegy on my God's marriage,

Tears in a best man's eyes,

Is like eclipse, a procrastination of moon, from glowing,

But my god is smiling,

So the eclipse doesn't matter,

Just like a tear in the best man's eyes,

Fatal distress, lit, wore black,

Ashes fell, smoke flew,

And levitation of psychedelic,

Glasses of hallucinating memories,

Memorial of memories, to hundreds, to read,

Just like a tear in the best man's eyes,

Flew in greed, to months long lilac skies to repeat,

Lament of best man, bled in black, indeed,

Sobriety ended,

Vows had just begun,

Mess of tear and blood, doesn't matter,

Just like my God's pledge of staying together,

Procrastinating eclipse, and best man's tear,

Worth just a view,

But twisted vows between god and goddess,

A worth to remember.

XV

Honeymoon.

Shall be poetess, of his happiness,

But dried august leaf burns faster than a paper,

It can't hold a dew, none of any weights it ever could,

In your shining daydreams, but your nightmares shall made of bloody veil,

Screams of your pardon, shall be overheard,

Just like a love you overshadowed,

Sinned off your beautiful features,

Taking away, what belongs to someone else,

You be now cursed for life, by the ached,

Aching hearts of feelings, ace of spade,

Conviction, of dryness, turning in garland,

Corsage of prom just mere, now written off,

Relish on feast of water, you get,

A day shall surpass, take you along, but dead,

Prolong this void wedding would be!?

On your marriage day, I wish groom kisses the best man, instead;

Wicked, your dreams of suited man kissing,

Vivid scar on a body, who loved the groom,

Black roses corseted, round your waist,

Condolencing to your dead love,

Holding on forest of August still had honeymoon,

Gold fire, and the beloved groom,

Nightmares collided in daydreams,

It all, at last came true.

XVI

An Un-(Written) August Memory.

Deeper silences of the grey sky,

Hold a ballad, in ode, triumph to dead,

Million poets die, poetry stays,

Where stars shine!? See in those words,

Reflections shan't get you back,

Of nothing is transparent at all, anyway,

Some shall weep,

I shall forever mourn,

Dreams collided in nightmares,

Now just sky is mere grey,

Story of clouds, shan't be understood by you,

It's deep in emotions to, get by feelingless,

Sand on our shoulders,

Jacket held my heart in, after all,

When you were there,

My brain erasing a written memory of August,

Unwritten song sung over violins,

Erasing, like twice strong my heart had gotten,

Brain, made it seemed a breeze,

But all my heart felt was a blizzard,

Slipping away in mere grey,

Got lost on someother way,

Tried to hold together; it all, fell apart,

Held fears so tight; scared my heart,

A written memory of August,

Was being unwritten.

XVII

Folded Paper.

Through lights in night, I glide fingers,

Through, light, the night ambiguous obscurity,

Loneliness is a fire, falling,

Pleading in hot nights, slightly colder,

I beg, shall stay, for I need, what's fading,

Glee of nothing, I still hold, to breakdowns, I hide,

To what stop!? To what shall begin!?

You stood on rose red exile,

As I see through blood tears, I cried for,

I wrote, for you, to let those fade in slate-grey!?

Screaming midst of folded paper,

Undressed dream, came true!?

For you, were never hesitant to stay,

But too firm to blur,

Was folded paper too scary, for you to read!?

A string to my neck, choking to die,

I wait for death, not too closely,

Sorry, for I caged, who wanted to be free.

XVIII

Blank Space.

Whole of it to gleam, in dark,

When till one shall endure!?

Pains, arrive waited long, on one,

This drives, drifts us apart,

Needn't have to have a power,

To let lilies, burn in fire of blood,

Whole of it to gleam, in dark,

Strove to blank spaces be filled,

Not by blood, by love, loyalty indeed,

Thrive in name of it, bliss to feel, hold on to it if you find it,

Young blood races,

Alluring in mysteries of dense shades,

If we were to gloom, wouldn't mind,

Until, to lift up each other we lived upto, promises,

When till one shall endure!? Sufferings alone,

In young blood that races, someone left behind,

Holding onto memories,

Pains, arrive waited long, on one,

Alluring in mysteries of dense shades,

Moon through glades, metaphors emphasized,

Dense shades an ecstasy of darkness, with you,

Alluring, mysteries of something, with you,

This drives, drifts us apart,

Needn't have to have a power,

To let lilies, burn in fire of blood,

Whole of it was love, attached with no conditions.

XIX

Middle Of Nowhere.

Halt, ache new, aurora in desert,

Oasis, mirage of unsettled subtle signs,

Lefts and rights of middle of nowhere,

Growls of pains, to no one has yet understood,

Stood on a side of view, clear,

Heartbreaks a weather of distress, discolor,

Halt, ache new, aurora in desert,

Aches of forceful smile, yet tears bottled,

Desert a heart of feelings ran dry, long ago,

To halt on a new pain on deserted heart,

Where, shall learn the art to let go!? When,

Oasis, mirage of unsettled subtle signs,

Hits too hard to break, stitches to wounds,

Stitched too closely to ache a more, no less to feel a breath,

To sides to stand, no eyes to stare,

Hundreds of them, only one made me scare,

Real of it, call love a despair,

Lefts and rights of middle of nowhere,

Shall scream to let lose a weight,

To go off to be a little insane,

Precisely no one learns to handle, someone,

Relationship with death my revival ascertain,

Growls of pains, to no one has yet understood,

Adjective to portray my desires,

Rather just address me a slut,

Just spare me emotional misconduct,

Stood on a side of view, clear,

Heartbreaks a weather of distress, discolor,

Pale in a casket, in middle of nowhere,

Carve, "by Love Be A Despair" on my headstone.

XX Peace.

And, what became of me, unknown,

No graves to evil shall be praised of,

Peace drawn off silver, ashes so black,

Too this sky cried, so wrath of ocean,

No August parch, dried, sepia,

Every vulnerable left crying, twice the scars,

And, what became of me, unknown,

Naked, over blood, off so done with light,

Fingers pierce, leaves poems on read,

To, what shall I become, unknown let it be,

No graves to evil shall be praised of,

Cupid be held for bloody silent mess,

Keister to be fucked, by despairing love,

No lie to stand, much to hate, pale grieve,

Peace drawn off silver, ashes so black,

Blue, midst grey, light golden, an august pale,

Laid back so silent, let mourning, voice the chorus,

Grey, to turn red, let imagination run wild, dead,

Too this sky cried, so wrath of ocean,

Forest of August, violins for peace ceremony,

Sky deep grey,

Afraid of, closing by, goodbye,

No August parch, dried, sepia,

Every vulnerable left crying, twice the scars,

Thereby, no sound, thereof, no remorse,

To let vulnerable crying, to let aching pain burn,

No lie to stand, much to hate, pale grieve,

A sound of relief, someone's mourns on someone's death,

To the dead, no death shall haunt,

Yet, to forget, the dead, shall silently sob.

XXI

Seven Heavens Much!?

Avalanche, discordant voices, twenty-five,

Roses, August, yet red, gleam,

Gloss, mirrors been bleeding, off loathing,

Seeming golden light, smoke covered, heat unfolding,

Broken, no testimonials,

Left dooming, yet leaving him immortal,

Avalanche, disaster, to a way, lead,

Discordant voices, screams for aches, to calm,

To twenty-five, meant no sense of harm,

Roses, August, yet red, gleam,

Gleam, shine through deep, a bone on seen,

August, flesh, soulless, in roses, a mirage,

Yet red, bone, and so did roses,

Gloss, mirrors been bleeding, off loathing,

March, gainst' August memories,

March a peace, match seven heavens,

August a dried forest, a seven hells,

Seeming golden light, smoke covered, heat unfolding,

Call it March, a heaven,

Or single stuck soul, August, a hell,

Smoke, off cigarette, in pain, or in love deep,

Broken, no testimonials,

Yet breaking, future seems unclear,

Testimonials, to shall leave a justified closure,

Broken, ever been, this dooming, or merrier!?

Left dooming, yet leaving him immortal,

Rather us, to bask in busk for heaven ways,

Or signs to show hell is the other way,

Yet leaving him immortal, in poems, letters a
vulnerable heaven and hell, of a life so anxious.

XXII

Blush Bear!

Cold, mascara eyes, woven blood strings,

Massacre, transcend, crescent,

Dazed, lullaby, hell too cries,

Blue, breath, indentation,

Stained graveyard sky,

Broken headstone, what's alive!?

Cold, mascara eyes, woven blood strings,

Hostage cuffed to my muffled pleads,

Numb, blood strings, woven intertwined,

Cold, sabotaged black pupil'd mascara eyes,

Massacre, transcend, crescent,

Massacre, transcend to crescent,

Massacre of longed still, too oblivious!?

Too easy, to massacre, but too hard to complete a crescent,

Dazed, lullaby, hell too cries,

Thought I would be caught in infidelity,

But I was caught in infidelity,

Lullaby, hell too cries, been dazed,

Blue, breath, indentation,

Blue your name,

Baby, I look gorgeous in blue and black,

Breath gone, sinking leaving an indentation,

I can see my death in peripheral,

Twined with my past,

The red, the blue, and your new white,

I blushed you roar in silences, kept unheard,

What love, to be loved, by lover,

When dead body to be loved by lover, unloved,

Stained graveyard sky,

Broken headstone, what's alive!?

XXIII
The Burning Room.

The burning room,

Confetti ashes of a burning,

Claustrophobia, jazz blue dripping,

Lines swirling, flames chocking,

Heat gauze, throne,

Chains on seventh layer skin,

Confetti ashes of a burning,

Siren of ambulance, on skin city,

Body on cliff, sliver being, blazing to bone,

Confessions spilt, bells tolling,

Claustrophobia, jazz blue dripping,

Spirit dances, of a jazz blue ever seen,

Knit strong, lips bleeding,

Unaware, blue vodka, high, haven't I ever seen,

Lines swirling, flames chocking,

A last tear ever cried,

On bail, no, a heart never stopped beating,

Lines swirling, to closure, has there ever been!?

Heat gauze, throne,

Melting faith, silences of scars, never unmade,

To sit, exclaim sigh, midst of orange sky,

White book, remains white, letters vulnerable to read,

Chains on seventh layer skin,

Comma, before stop, exclaim fore' question,

Aftermath, delay of emotions to cope,

Fireflies, on roof, to scene being burn,

The burning room,

Let alone, end chapter ran March till August,

Delays till, December, in immortal history,

Shall no soul to haunt, no ash to fall,

Over someone that saw no one burn,

In The burning room.

XXIV

Unsaturated.

Rock bottom, of infinity, unclear,

Rust, colour of solitude, on neck,

Through gaze in deep, sheer disgrace, bleeds,

Red island of roses, turns red roses black,

Possession of me through light, still on lease,

Dismantle peace, pieces in breath,

Rock bottom, of infinity, unclear,

Rough silences midst claustrophobia of emptiness,

Graves, vision unsaturated,

Grey scale, mid white unbalance over black,

Rust, colour of solitude, on neck,

Morning after death shall be of solitude,

Looking through, how would he feel,

Pale hue of grey, not so deep,

Possession of me through light, still on lease,

Dismantle peace, pieces in breath,

Through gaze, in-deep sheer disgrace, bleeds,

Leaves over grave, of mid, august so parched,

Red island of roses, turns red roses black,

Fingers through dark, over lights embark,

Left aside, in pieces of dismantle peace,

Possession of me through light, still on lease.

XXV
Echoes Of Sawdust.

Thesis of infinity, stops,

Flesh, pain to bones, mere blood,

Bedroom floor, spotlight, eyes lone echoes,

Screams pauses, righteous, to us holy, love,

Where shall it all, we begin!?

Eyes shut, and my crumpled faith, builds,

Thesis of infinity, stops,

Suffice, my unmade, mare pants on bed,

Groans of superficial lust,

Indecisive young'd, feeling in heart, reputed,

Flesh, pain to bones, mere blood,

Rung church bells, reputation of using unused,

Mused, eyes, where lone echoes, undust,

Body of saw dust, might now unrust, of mine,

Bedroom floor, spotlight, eyes lone echoes,

Cigarettes burning, silk sheets now tangled,

Kisses serenading, uncelebrated,

Dick pierces in and through, self ruptured,

Where shall it all, we begin!?

Eyes shut, and my crumpled faith, builds,

Lose oneself, over just a touch of another,

Screams pauses, righteous, to us holy, love.

Flesh, pain to bones, mere blood,

Thesis of infinity, stops,

Bedroom floor, spotlight, eyes lone echoes,

Screams pauses, righteous, to us holy, love,

Temple, in my brain, made on skin, I preach,

Rung church bells, reputation of using unused,

Mused, in my eyes, touch healing the burns,

It's righteous, your dick through me, I call love.

XXVI

Cry Shoulder.

Sorry, bitter scars cry, bleed for beloved,

Within or amidst silences, buried,

Craves for misery, carves still; band-aid lullaby,

To whispers, be whimsical, shall what, let be!?

Honor, of fallen king, walked over,

Charisma, wounded blood dry,

Sorry, bitter scars cry, bleed for beloved,

Bitter scars of cry shoulder, bleeds yet,

Bleeds for beloved, to fall for, acceptance,

Sorry, apology, for paradise burnt at stake,

Within or amidst silences, buried,

Yet gets gloomy alone,

Silences, white noise, fading static adoration,

Care, within or amidst silences, blurry buried,

Craves for misery, carves still; band-aid lullaby,

Misery of a young failing again and again,

Carves still, a cry shoulder,

Band-aid lullaby, to misery, affection of twenty-five,

To whispers, be whimsical, shall what, let be!?

Be there wide eye awake,

Shall what whimsical mean!? In any whispers,

Thereby,

Let be hope, neath' sorries,

Honor, of fallen king, walked over,

Charisma, wounded blood dry,

Now eulogizing a mortal, into immortality,

Yet no apologies more than a blur,

Sorry, apology, for paradise burnt at stake,

Yet gets gloomy alone,

Misery of a young failing again and again,

Be there wide eye awake,

Cry shoulder to be,

Let be, bitter scars there-about,

Longing still, a bliss; for eternity,

Fallen king, in valley of prince, psychotic.

XXVII

The Fallen King.

So forth, soil in amendments,

At nightfall, withstand, or withdraw,

Touch, don't forbid, peal for pearls,

Stand or leave, awhile, reimburse,

Emotions locked, young fallen old,

Sightstuck, skeleton'd soul,

So forth, soil in amendments,

To grow, to not stop, at all a point,

So forth, upright madness, magic hell,

Amendments togetherness forever more,

At nightfall, withstand, or withdraw,

Fever like a beast, stop, break a delicate,

To withstand at glade, to withdraw abrupt,

Might think at nightfall,

Touch, don't forbid, peal for pearls,

Seek rights, to incarnate,

For a touch, longstill,

Once for all, never do forbid, peal for pearls,

Stand or leave, awhile, reimburse,

Peal, for a body, would remain unsung,

Pearls, through glide, for soul, stuck within skeleton,

To stand, or to never leave for a while to reimburse,

Emotions locked, young fallen old,

Sightstuck, skeleton'd soul,

Locked, sealed by kiss,

Fallen old by sightstuck, on the fallen king.

XXVIII

Death Potion.

Atrocities, extremities,

Shines, shivers, severe sacrifice,

Eyes, enchantment, empty elite destiny,

Ink, illusions, infatuation, illness ignite,

Lament, lay, lingers, lower, neath' love comes from,

Disgrace, deals open eyes, forever,

Atrocities, a lie, glittery eyes,

Distorted mosaic vision,

Extremities, of love, let's lose pale,

Shattered, a sane, old, lost to bane,

Shines, shivers, severe sacrifice,

Shivers, of loosing,

Shines, horrific mares, off reflections,

By, severe sacrifice, mind and heart,

Eyes, enchantment, empty elite destiny,

Cautious to be in conscious,

Eyes, enchanted, by euphony, of features,

Empty elite destiny, of someone toy'd with,

Ink, illusions, infatuation, illness ignite,

Ailing birthed by hallucinations,

Illusions, of beauty, be destined,

Ink, illness ignites, satire to anxiety, attacks makes her perspire,

Lament, lay, lingers, lower, neath' love comes from,

Howls of aches no meant to be heard by,

Hate, lay, lingers, from lowest my love ignited from,

Lament, shall too, breathe, somewhere below,

Disgrace, deals open eyes, forever,

Her eyes, my lips, her hands, my face,

Shall be left to haunt to pass you the nights,

Atrocities, extremities of love, makes sane, insane,

Cautious to be in conscious,

Howls of aches no meant to be heard by,

Ailing birthed by hallucinations,

To calm, to be, by death potion itself.

XXIX disgust.

Ashes won't formulate to bones again,

If ballads are made of pain,

Misogyny is so pale,

The I wish time shall wait awhile,

Disgust, they find in nicotine,

Then when would tears come and halt!?

Why would love tangle in sheets!?

Is it illicit, or explicit!?

When, I shall write, feelings shall be in quarantine,

If not, then where has the real love been!?

Perception a sieve for judgements,

Then humanity found itself in spiral of disdain,

If not, then why gay love, amends!?

Find flowing back to vain, with regards of being insane,

Disgust of smoke floating in air,

Then creation of a different world shall begin,

Dark sunshine,

Cohesiveness of feelings,

Mistaken, for human damages,

Lips, tastes different, if bitten in interest,

Horizon in bed,

Where oasis shall quench two hearts,

Farther where broken glasses, should mend,

Whilst of hate, love ignites, like incense.

XXX

Self Harm.

Black satin, maroon, vivid,

Red, fear, flags, glasses broken lens,

Obsession, pure deluxe, desire, death,

Charm, chains, champagne'd lips,

Ignite nostalgia, torn empathy, resides,

Camouflage, outlaw'd, urges revival, sigh, exclaim,

Black satin, maroon, vivid,

Shall what skies cry about!?

Black satin, my skin bestowed in,

Maroon, blood heart, memories vivid,

Red, fear, flags, glasses broken lens,

To beyond a breath, heavens await,

Hell a red fear, trauma, being left alone of,

Flags red, glasses broken lens, of love,

Obsession, pure deluxe, desire, death,

Hell to be there, fire of pure love dismantle at stake,

Obsession, infatuation, pure deluxe,

Desires lead nowhere but to death, of love,

Charm, chains, champagne'd lips,

Heaven shall lead, to continue lies to you,

Charm, of someone chaotic calm,

Chains, on my wrist, and champagne'd lips,

Shall what skies cry about!?

To beyond a breath, heavens await,

Hell to be there, fire of pure love dismantle at stake,

Heaven shall lead, to continue lies to you,

Ignite nostalgia, torn empathy, resides,

Haven't I have self harmed, to die,

But to forget the pains,

To believe I mustn't have been the one, you deserve,

Camouflage, outlaw'd, urges revival, sigh, exclaim,

To hallucinate you, shall stop,

When outlaw'd you, affect me still be camouflaged,

Being urged a revival, to sigh relieve, exclaim fore' a stop.

XXXI

A Last Tear Ever Cried.

Forgotten, forgiven, forsaken our existence,

Beheld by darkness, uphold tears,

Longing still, droughted skin, craves hugs,

Bruised, apprehensive, instance of existence,

Destine of mansion, her slave, I congratulate,

Our memories, lullaby, I commemorate,

Forgotten, forgiven, forsaken our existence,

To live upon the streets of haze, memories,

Cologne of your chest, a smile, I've forgotten,

Forgiven sins, under prophecy of love,

Beheld by darkness, uphold tears,

Pronunciation of us, proclamation of feelings,

Darkness to bow, to uphold tears,

Just a journey to my salvation,

Destine of mansion, her slave, I congratulate,

Our memories, lullaby, I commemorate,

Longing still, droughted skin, craves hugs,

Unlike her destiny, my fate, too, longed still, to feel,

Bruised, apprehensive, instance of existence,

Un-merry choirs of angels, sung off key,

Our memories, lullaby, I commemorate with,

A last tear I ever cry.

XXXII

Writings On the Wall.

Writings on the wall,

I read on an august midday,

Precisely, remember, what it read,

I shall quote it, but I ignore,

Let still; my love, be for the one,

Not for nobody now exists,

Sacred feelings, I shall drain em' on the one,

Nothing never lasted, redeeming everlasting,

Old love if I remember, won't be crying,

Reminiscing the falling, deep,

If I smile, wouldn't be on memories,

But on my idiocracy,

You're that august dry, lovers rustle leaves in,

Written in hundredth pop song,

Lovers will be making out thereby,

Shall I bent down, or sing the lyric of the night,

Feelings never die, so my love ever won't,

Ceaseful my silence be,

Fading feelings you perceive, if I shall speak,

I would always would be harsh and sweet,

"Let still; my love, be for the one,

Old love if I remember, won't be crying,

You're that august dry, lovers rustle leaves in,

Feelings never die, so my love ever won't"

Precisely, remember, what it read,

I shall quote it, but I ignore.

XXXIII

Gentle Peace.

Slow, a gentle peace, glides through,

Abrupt, pause, second guessing,

Arteries burst, combustion in chambers,

Faded false fireflies of fiction,

Ruptures by friction,

Plea, unsolicited by someone at all,

Slow, a gentle peace, glides through,

Silence an echo, to someone, something he owe,

Gentle peace, a try, to put scars on peace,

Glides through, slow, and mellow,

Abrupt, pause, second guessing,

No harms to mean, to flesh, to let soul free,

Abrupt, pause, to second guess to let me be me,

By a power, for superficial loner to be free,

Arteries burst, combustion in chambers,

To let be, or to let go,

Combustion, chaos, of overthinking,

In chambers of feelings, where no hate be,

Faded false fireflies of fiction,

No real scene, never been,

Fireflies a love, fictions made it seem,

Now all it be, faded, false, and fickle,

Ruptures by friction,

Plea, unsolicited by someone at all,

No time meant to make anxious,

Only if anxiety shall breathe, I choose to be let free.

XXXIV

Starvation To Salvation.

Whining for a breath of peace,

Grinding, for a day, shall not be in afterglow,

Subliming, your faith,

Residue, would be desire to grow,

A sigh right now, shall be,

Whirlwind of Salvation after all,

Moon is overrated,

Just like these words, from an anonymous,

Clouds would be greater hustles,

Than what shines off reflections,

Wailing, shall now rest in peace,

Honors to priority shall begin,

Angels won't mourn, on devil's exit,

Forgiven, now forbidden, lows would exit,

Only then your,

Starvation to Salvation, convert,

Anonymous poet of this poem,

Shall wish your soul to find peace,

Not only in afterlife, soul finds peace,

In this eternity, your soul too, will,

Long awaited revival, shall begin,

Quieten camouflaged happiness,

Reflect that old sorrow of time, dead,

Then,

Your starvation to salvation,

Will succeed.

XXXV

Goodbye.

Coughing, conjured, by anxiety,

Less regards, to eyelids weight,

You let me bleed off white, opaque sight to soul,

Sire, of me, now ashes cling to air in open space to breathe,

Wear cologne to sooth atmosphere, bleak,

Over a head hover clouds of future misty,

Coughing, conjured, by anxiety,

To place shall this body return to,

Houses, a homeland of known, to be safe,

Implored by anxiety, more of a demand imposed,

Coughing a metaphor,

To shall not throw words, rather been gulped,

To be guilty, of something imaginative yet not done,

Coughing, metaphor to woe, words unsaid,

Less regards, to eyelids weight,

Feelings to not roll down, not again,

Eyelids, as if were shoulders to feelings,

Weights of past not been dead,

You let me bleed off white, opaque sight to soul,

Indebted to lessons taught,

Unaware of some feels, farthermore, awaits by hands of future,

Off white my semen's bled, some nights off aches, some of joy,

Sire, of me, now ashes cling to air in open space to breathe,

Wear cologne to sooth atmosphere, bleak,

Over a head hover clouds of future misty,

Shall not anymore spend time gulping pain,

Coughing, metaphor to woe, words unsaid,

Goodbye, never been easy,

But harder by standing on broken heart,

Memories cry, and I whisper, Goodbye.

XXXVI

Throat Bone.

Faded yellow happiness,

Tangible, obscure serene,

Cynical chuckles, choking,

Wisteria, blooded illusion,

Serpentine of burgundy to brown,

Hailstones tilting halo,

Faded yellow happiness,

Sepia churchyard wedding,

Blush rose, tears, inevitable,

Beautiful day indeed,

Tangible, obscure serene,

Burnt moon paradise,

Tangible misery, musings

An obscure serene,

Cynical chuckles, choking,

Cynical chuckles, toxicity,

Levitating on skies of seven birth dreams,

Chocking, claustrophobic corseted, throat;

Kintsugi, clay body,

Golden, cigarette, broken bridges, centerfolds,

To heaven and to hell,

Nightfall, blinded by, I, falling apart, in;

Wisteria, blooded illusion,

Blooded illusion ceremony,

Wisterias, on my ethereal room,

Drying tears, cotton to my wounds,

Serpentine of burgundy to brown,

Mustard yellow happiness, faded,

Serpentine of red, to burgundy,

Brown, burns my blood to,

Hailstones tilting halo,

Hailstones to my forehead,

Shatters my halo to earth,

Blue, in no time turns, my skin, vaporize, soul.

XXXVII
Apple Garden.

Cantillation carnation, comatose,

Vineyards, barrel fields, smiles,

Addiction, disease, desperation,

Whine, devouring, bloody hands,

Apple garden, shredded shroud,

Grey sky, perseverance, mistress,

Cantillation carnation, comatose,

Cantillating ruthless, distorted peace,

Carnation limerence,

Instead ruthless comatose,

Vineyards, barrel fields, smiles,

Sunset on a vineyard,

Black corset on a graveyard,

The lakes, home to dead poets, left on;

Addiction, disease, desperation,

Contemporary addiction, of skin cologne,

Wrapped around in a diction,

Disease a desperation, you, shan't fall,

Whine, devouring, bloody hands,

Whine, to stop blood to bleed,

Bloody hands, forever, and evermore,

Your foolery was a shenanigan planned,

Apple garden, shredded shroud,

Blood drops, psychotic, distorted whine,

Fathom, why!? Forbidden apple garden, sighs,

Hearts shatter, does that happen everytime!?

Grey sky, perseverance, mistress,

Grey sky, your misery ending to goodbye!?

Perseverance, to stay, while mistress, dancing,

Pounding yet drowning, in itself,

"All of my poetries are available on the streaming servives as audiobook, produced and recorded by me."

thank-you!
really means a lot.

9 798888 151679